The Gospel of the Resurrection
The Good News About How Jesus Defeated Death

Cody Cook

2020
Cants Firmus Media

This essay may be freely copied and distributed, so long as the author's name and website address is retained. If you would like a shareable, digital version of this work, you are welcome to visit www.cantus-firmus.com

Scripture quotations, unless otherwise noted, are from the ESV® Bible (The Holy Bible, English Standard Version®), copyright © 2001 by Crossway, a publishing ministry of Good News Publishers. Used by permission. All rights reserved.

Scripture quotations marked (NASB) taken from the New American Standard Bible®, Copyright © 1960, 1962, 1963, 1968, 1971, 1972, 1973, 1975, 1977, 1995 by The Lockman Foundation. Used by permission.

1st print edition
2nd digital edition

ISBN-13 9781652441397

"Since therefore the children share in flesh and blood, he himself likewise partook of the same things, that through death he might destroy the one who has the power of death, that is, the devil, and deliver all those who through fear of death were subject to lifelong slavery."
Hebrews 2:14-15

The Gospel of the Resurrection

Foreword
by Christopher M. Date

The early church father Tertullian wrote, "there is nobody who lives so much in accordance with the flesh as they who deny the resurrection of the flesh."[1] Perhaps his words apply also to those Christians who might believe in resurrection but don't really yearn for it. I have become convinced that many or most of my fellow Christians look forward to going to heaven when they die more than they long for being raised from the dead immortal—if they think about resurrection, or even believe in it, at all. This may explain why the church today, in many parts of the world, looks lamentably like the world when it comes to a number of moral issues.

---

[1] Tertullian, *On the Resurrection of the Flesh*, 11.

This is what spurred me to enter earnestly into ministry in 2009, when I still believed the view of hell I was taught when I became a Christian early that decade. It wasn't until two years later, in 2011, that I was challenged with, and was ultimately persuaded by, the biblical evidence for conditional immortality. Still, even then it did not occur to me that the church's seeming ignorance and underappreciation of resurrection might be connected to its widespread acceptance of eternal torment, a view which teaches that *everyone* will be raised bodily immortal and will live physically forever (albeit not all in the same neighborhood, as it were).

In this short but powerful work, Cody Cook helpfully unpacks this connection and shows how the Bible's consistent message, from Old Testament to New, is that fallen human beings must be saved through faith in Jesus Christ if they are to escape death in resurrection. The gospel is not meant to rescue sinners from one future life, lived forever in miserable separation from God, unto another future life, lived forever in blissful communion with him. No, the gospel is about saving lives altogether, rescuing sinners from certain death by granting them resurrected, eternal life in the community of God's redeemed people. I am confident that this will become clear to open-minded readers of Cook's

The Gospel of the Resurrection

essay who are willing to put their traditions to the biblical test, and I suspect that those whose eyes are so opened will experience life-transformation unlike most anything they have undergone before.

Cody Cook

Introduction

The reformed theologian and apologist James White has remarked on more than one occasion that the man who thinks he has no traditions is in fact a slave to his traditions.

That's why when it comes to reading the Bible, we often miss its message and instead find in it exactly what we've been told we will by our pastor, denomination, or our favorite celebrity preacher. When our eyes scan passages which seem to contradict our pet theologies, we can gloss over them unless someone draws our attention to them.

It is the aim of this work to demonstrate that a major theme which runs throughout scripture, the mortality of human beings, has been obscured by a tradition—the inherent immortality of the human soul. Those who fail to recognize this biblical theme suffer from a severe malady indeed: they cannot see or understand the gospel message as it was presented by Jesus' earliest followers and have substituted a partial gospel in its place.

Contrary to what many of us have been told, the gospel preached by the apostles is a gospel of resurrection. While it would be overly simplistic to say that the gospel is *only* about resurrection, it is an essential component of it that we have left out. It's high time we retrieved it.

But before we can demonstrate that, we'll need to start in the Old Testament. These scriptures explain to us the trouble we find ourselves in—the bad news that makes the good news so good.

The Old Testament on Human Mortality

The Bible begins with an account of human beings as the creation of God. Its first book, the book of Genesis, emphasizes that not only are Adam and Eve made by God and are therefore dependent in this sense, but their continued existence is entirely dependent upon being in right relationship with Him. Disobedience and faithlessness on man's part severed the ties between man and God, and as a result removed the possibility of perpetual existence from mankind:

> "The LORD God commanded the man, saying, 'From any tree of the garden you may eat freely; but from the tree of the knowledge of good and evil you shall not eat, for in the

day that you eat from it you will surely die'" (Genesis 2:16-17, NASB).

Dr. Glenn Peoples provides this commentary of the passage:

> "God tells Adam not to eat of the tree of the knowledge of good and evil, or he would die (literally, 'dying you shall die'). [The theologian John] Calvin was right, I think, to see that this means not that man would drop dead on the day that he ate, but that Adam's death commenced on that day and culminated on the day that he returned to the dust, just as God promised. Commenting on this verse, he said, 'The miseries and evils both of soul and body, with which man is beset so long as he is on earth, are a kind of entrance into death, till death itself entirely absorbs him.' As we know, the first humans did rebel against God, and God judged them. The serpent had told Eve that in spite of God's warning, in fact they would not die. They would gain knowledge, and lose nothing (Gen. 3:4-5). As the story unfolds, we see that this was a lie. In Genesis 3:22 we see that God would not allow sinful man to remain alive indefinitely."[2]

---

[2] Glenn Peoples, "Why I am an Annihilationist." Accessed via

The Gospel of the Resurrection

Peoples' conclusion highlights the response of God in Genesis 3:22 to Adam and Eve's falling into disobedience: the eating of the forbidden fruit did not bring death directly but triggered a response from God. He banished humanity from His life-sustaining presence in Eden:

> "Then the LORD God said, 'Behold, the man has become like one of us in knowing good and evil. Now, lest he reach out his hand and take also of the tree of life and eat, and live forever—'"

God doesn't finish the sentence. A world in which sinful creatures cannot be destroyed but go on perpetually tainting God's creation is too horrible to even discuss. It is worth noting that this verse wouldn't make sense if Adam and Eve were immortal by nature. Indeed, it assumes that they were not, but that immortality for humans was conditioned upon God granting it to them. After humanity fell away from the purposes which God created them for, letting them live forever would be destructive to God's creation.

Thus, following Adam and Eve's disobedience, they were removed from the source of life. After being thrown out of the Garden of Eden

---

http://www.rightreason.org/article/theology/annihilationist.pdf

and banished from eating of the tree of life, pain and death followed.[3] In other words, God takes away His sustaining power so that man will die and return to the dirt he was made from.

The 4th century church father Athanasius, known in the annals of church history as the father and protector of Christian orthodoxy, gives a similar interpretation of the Eden account in his classic work *On the Incarnation*, where he argued that man is by nature mortal and that immortality is conditioned upon God's grace:

> "This, then, was the plight of men. God had not only made them out of nothing, but had also graciously bestowed on them His own life by the grace of the Word. Then, turning from eternal things to things corruptible, by counsel of the devil, they had become the cause of their own corruption in death; for, as I said before, though they were by nature subject to corruption, the grace of their union with the Word made them capable of escaping from the natural law, provided that they retained the beauty of innocence with

---

[3] The tree of life is brought back into the biblical narrative when God restores humanity in order to show that everlasting life has been given to us in Christ (Revelation 22:2), but we're getting ahead of ourselves.

which they were created."[4]

For the most part, the rest of the Old Testament assumes mortality for humans. Psalm 82, which gives a fascinating peek into the world of fallen angels, features a speech by God where he compares these divine beings to men—though they may be gods of a sort and sons of God, "nevertheless, like men [they] shall die" (82:7). The implication is that not only are angels *not* inherently immortal, they are like humans whose mortality is beyond question.

Likewise, Psalm 115:17 asserts, "the dead do not praise the Lord, nor do any who go down into silence" and Psalm 146 says of man, "when his breath departs, he returns to the earth; on that very day his plans perish." The author of Ecclesiastes is also probably reflecting the view of his countrymen when he says, "for the living know that they will die, but the dead know nothing, and they have no more reward, for the memory of them is forgotten" (Ecclesiastes 9:5). These passages bear out what Genesis 2-3 are claiming—man's natural fate, assuming that God does not intervene, is not immortality but annihilation.

---

[4] Athanasius, On the Incarnation, 1:5. Accessed via http://www.ccel.org/ccel/athanasius/incarnation

Cody Cook

"Hell" in the Old Testament

Of course some Bible translations, in particular the King James Version, do speak of "hell" as the fate of some humans who die. Doesn't this demonstrate that the Old Testament does claim eternal conscious torment as the inevitable fate of the wicked?

Not at all! The Hebrew word sometimes translated "hell" is *"sheol,"* a word which can refer to the grave (Genesis 37:35, 1 Kings 2:6, Psalm 6:5, Isaiah 15:9), a pit (Numbers 16:30), a great depth (Deuteronomy 32:22, Job 11:8), and sometimes figuratively to death or destruction (2 Samuel 22:6, Job 26:6).

It is used in parallel constructions with death (2 Samuel 22:6, Psalm 6:5, Psalm 55:15, Psalm 89:49, Proverbs 5:5, Isaiah 28:15, Hosea 13:14), darkness (Job 17:13), dust (Job 17:16), destruction (Job 26:6, Proverbs 15:11, Proverbs 27:20), and corruption (Psalm 16:10). It is contrasted with life (Psalm 89:48, Proverbs 15:24). Therefore, since *sheol* is so strongly connected with destruction, it is very misleading to translate it with a word like hell which generally suggests a place of eternal conscious torment to modern ears.

There is, admittedly, one passage about a

pagan king being brought down to *sheol* which has similarities to how the later doctrine of hell is sometimes articulated as a place of conscious existence:

> "*Sheol* beneath is stirred up to meet you when you come; it rouses the shades to greet you, all who were leaders of the earth; it raises from their thrones all who were kings of the nations. All of them will answer and say to you: 'You too have become as weak as we! You have become like us!' Your pomp is brought down to *Sheol*, the sound of your harps; maggots are laid as a bed beneath you, and worms are your covers" (Isaiah 14:9-11).

Though the picture painted is of conscious existence, this passage's poetic genre might suggest that it would be better understood as figurative language for the grave. The rest of the passage's imagery only strengthens this assumption. For instance, the kings who welcome their comrade speak of their relative weakness compared to their living existence, their being surrounded in darkness, and the maggots and worms which are present in the grave. The point Isaiah is seeking to make is not that life continues after death, but that even those who glory in their power will be brought to nothing when they meet their demise—despite the pagan myths of kings ascending to deity after their deaths.

Cody Cook

Hints of Immortality

While death is treated as the normal and expected end for human beings, there are a number of possible allusions to life after death in the Old Testament, as well as at least one direct reference to it. In all of these examples, life after death is entirely conditional upon the will of God. It is not described as something that can be simply expected on the basis of essential human immortality. For instance, Psalm 37 might be claiming eternal life for God's true people, though clearly not for the wicked who will be "altogether destroyed":

> "For the Lord loves justice; he will not forsake his saints. They are preserved forever, but the children of the wicked shall be cut off. The righteous shall inherit the land and dwell upon it forever... Mark the blameless and behold the upright, for there is a future for the man of peace. But transgressors shall be altogether destroyed; the future of the wicked shall be cut off" (Psalm 37:28-29, 37-38).

Malachi, a later Hebrew prophet from around the 5th century B.C., also seems to be looking forward to the end of the age when he speaks of the fates of the wicked and the redeemed. Life and healing is promised for the righteous, but the language which describes the fate of the wicked is difficult to understand in any other sense but of utter annihilation:

> "For behold, the day is coming, burning like an oven, when all the arrogant and all evildoers will be stubble. The day that is coming shall set them ablaze, says the Lord of hosts, so that it will leave them neither root nor branch. But for you who fear my name, the sun of righteousness shall rise with healing in its wings. You shall go out leaping like calves from the stall. *And you shall tread down the wicked, for they will be ashes under the soles of your feet, on the day when I act*, says the Lord of hosts" (Malachi 4:1-3, emphasis mine).

Daniel 12:2 provides us with the strongest proof-text in the Old Testament for life after death. In it, the prophet refers to a future resurrection of both the redeemed and the wicked:

> "And many of those who sleep in the dust of the earth shall awake, some to everlasting life, and some to shame and everlasting contempt."

While Daniel doesn't clearly speak of destruction as the final fate of the wicked here, he also doesn't speak of eternal conscious torment—being the object of everlasting contempt does not require that one continue to exist forever.

The Old Testament set the scene for us. Part of the human problem is that we are heading toward death as the result of disunion with our Creator. These scriptures give glimmers of hope for those whom God has called His own, but the picture is still fuzzy. And yet in the prophet Isaiah, in the fifty-second and fifty-third chapters, we read of a man who was pierced for our transgressions and wounded to heal us—brought to the grave despite being completely innocent. And this same man who was put to death to give us peace is said to, as a result of taking our place in death, prolong his days. Who is this man who defeats death by being crushed on our behalf?

The Apostolic Presentation of the Good News

The New Testament affirms the Old Testament's view of death as the natural fate of man. Under normative circumstances, human beings will "perish" (John 3:16), "die" (John 6:50), receive death as the proper payment for their sin (Romans 6:23), etc. In contrast, "[God] alone possesses immortality" as a necessary quality of His being (1 Timothy 6:16).

Where then, does the Christian doctrine of eternal life come from? How did the apostles who wrote the New Testament defend their proclamation that God had rescued His people from death?

The apostle Peter's speech during the feast of Pentecost to his fellow Jews is the first recorded apostolic proclamation of the gospel after Jesus' death and resurrection. Here's his summary of the good news from that sermon:

> "This Jesus, delivered up according to the definite plan and foreknowledge of God, you crucified and killed by the hands of lawless men. God raised him up, loosing the pangs of death, because it was not possible for him to be held by it" (Acts 2:23-24).

In another gospel proclamation, Peter chastised his audience in this way: "and you killed the Author of life, whom God raised from the dead. To this we are witnesses" (Acts 3:15). The book of Acts goes on to reference the resurrection multiple times in its summaries of apostolic preaching (see 4:10, 10:40, 13:30-37, 17:3, 17:31, 26:22-23).

Moving past Peter, in 1 Corinthians 15 the apostle Paul repeats the apostolic teaching that was shared with him in credal form after he converted to Christian faith, highlighting the resurrection as part of the basic gospel teaching:

> "For I delivered to you as of first importance what I also received: that Christ died for our sins in accordance with the Scriptures, that he was buried, that he was raised on the third day in accordance with the Scriptures" (1

The Gospel of the Resurrection

Corinthians 15:3-4).

In one sense, the apostolic teaching of resurrection was not new. By this point in history a belief in a future resurrection had become popular among many Jews and was championed by the Pharisees (see Acts 24:15, 26:5-8). What made the gospel about Jesus different is that it claimed that Jesus' own resurrection is the necessary requirement for our resurrection unto life. We may only overcome death when we are joined to the God-man Jesus Christ who defeated death and thereby made resurrection unto eternal life possible for all men.

The church father Athanasius, whom we appealed to for our diagnosis of the problem, also was kind enough to give us the prescription for its cure:

> "[Through] union of the immortal Son of God with our human nature, all men were clothed with incorruption in the promise of the resurrection. For the solidarity of mankind is such that, by virtue of the Word's indwelling in a single human body, the corruption which goes with death has lost its power over all."[5]

---

[5] Athanasius, On the Incarnation, 2:9. Accessed via http://www.ccel.org/ccel/athanasius/incarnation

Jesus took on death and beat it. "Being raised from the dead, [He] will never die again; death no longer has dominion over him . . . but he lives to God" (Romans 6:9-10). That's why Jesus' resurrection factors into so many apostolic presentations of the gospel: it is the basis of the hope for our own resurrection.[6]

Paul's letters make this clear over and over again. For him, the good news has to do with humanity overcoming death through what God did in Jesus the God-man:

> "For if, because of one man's trespass [Adam], death reigned through that one man, much more will those who receive the abundance of grace and the free gift of righteousness reign in life through the one man Jesus Christ" (Romans 5:17).

"For the wages of sin is death, but the free gift of God is eternal life in Christ Jesus our Lord" (Romans 6:23).

"God [saved us] and called us to a holy calling, not because of our works but because

---

[6] It was also seen as having apologetic value, since the apostles reasoned that God would not have raised up a false messiah.

of his own purpose and grace, which he gave us in Christ Jesus before the ages began, and which now has been manifested through the appearing of our Savior Christ Jesus, who abolished death and brought life and immortality to light through the gospel" (2 Tim 1:9-10).

At the root of Paul's view of salvation is a mystical union with Christ. Because we are joined to Christ, we share in his death for sin (which provides forgiveness for our sins) as well as His resurrection unto eternal life. For example, in Romans 6:4-9 Paul says that when we were baptized into Christ, we were baptized into his death, so that:

"just as Christ was raised from the dead by the glory of the Father, we too might walk in newness of life. For if we have been united with him in a death like his, we shall certainly be united with him in a resurrection like his... Now if we have died with Christ, we believe that we will also live with him. We know that Christ, being raised from the dead, will never die again; death no longer has dominion over him" (See also Colossians 3:3-4, 2 Corinthians 5:17-18).

Paul argues here that because of Christ's resurrection, we can have confidence in being resurrected unto life if we are in Christ. Christ's resurrection is put forth as proof that death has been conquered by Him. We have also conquered death with Christ, but only if we are joined to Him. As Paul goes on to say that, "if the Spirit of him who raised Jesus from the dead dwells in you, he who raised Christ Jesus from the dead will also give life to your mortal bodies through his Spirit who dwells in you" (Romans 8:11).

The resurrection of Jesus was such a powerful event that it ultimately bifurcated humanity into two—one humanity united to Adam that is heading to death, and one united to Christ that looks forward to being resurrected. And just as the biblical Adam is the fount of the first humanity, Jesus is the source of the second:

> "But in fact Christ has been raised from the dead, the firstfruits of those who have fallen asleep. For as by a man came death, by a man has come also the resurrection of the dead. For as in Adam all die, so also in Christ shall all be made alive. But each in his own order: Christ the firstfruits, then at his coming those who belong to Christ. Then comes the end, when he delivers the kingdom to God the Father after destroying every rule and every authority and power. For he must reign until he has put all his enemies under his feet. The last enemy to be destroyed is death" (1 Corinthians 15:20-26. See also 2 Corinthians

2:16).

Paul has no hope in resurrection apart from Jesus, praying as he does that by union with Christ he hopes to "attain the resurrection from the dead" (Philippians 3:11), relying on "God who raises the dead" (2 Corinthians 1:9), namely those "who have been brought from death to life" (Romans 6:13).

The writer of the epistle to the Hebrews likewise sees the defeat of death as central to Jesus' mission. The reason Jesus shared in our flesh and blood was so that He "might destroy the one who has the power of death, that is, the devil, and deliver all those who through fear of death were subject to lifelong slavery" (2:14-15). Jesus "tasted death" for us so that He might bring us out of it and into "glory" (2:9-10). In sum, Jesus joined His divine nature to our human so that He could face death on our behalf, beat it, and elevate our human nature so that we might become sons of God united to Him as Jesus' human and divine natures are united together (John 17:21-23).

This doctrine of a resurrection unto life being for the redeemed alone is not only in Paul. Jesus makes this claim as well:
> "The sons of this age marry and are given in marriage, but those who are considered worthy to attain to that age and to the

resurrection from the dead neither marry nor are given in marriage, for they cannot die anymore, because they are equal to angels and are sons of God, being sons of the resurrection." (Luke 20:34-36).

Jesus tells us that one must be worthy to attain unto the resurrection of life, which results in them being incapable of dying. In John's Gospel, Jesus makes the claim that the aforementioned worthiness for eternal life is measured by whether or not someone has Christ in them:

> "I am the bread of life. Your fathers ate the manna in the wilderness, and they died. This is the bread that comes down from heaven, so that one may eat of it and not die. I am the living bread that came down from heaven. If anyone eats of this bread, he will live forever. And the bread that I will give for the life of the world is my flesh" (John 6:48-51).

Finally, John, reflecting on Jesus' earthly mission, summarizes the gospel message through a life versus death dichotomy very familiar to what we've found in the New Testament up to this point:

> "For God so loved the world, that he gave his only Son, that whoever believes in him should not perish but have eternal life" (John 3:16).

The Gospel of the Resurrection

One interesting feature of the New Testament teaching of resurrection is that it often tends to give the impression that the damned won't be resurrected at all. Note that in Luke 20:34-38, the resurrection unto life is simply referred to as "the resurrection of the dead," even though the context makes it clear that the passage is referring to the resurrection of only those who are "worthy."

Perhaps the reason for this is that whether the damned are temporarily raised or not, their ultimate fate is utter destruction and annihilation, so their resurrection is simply not comparable to the resurrection of the redeemed. Elsewhere in the New Testament, the damned are described as being raised up, but only for the purpose of judgment:

> "An hour is coming when all who are in the tombs will hear his voice and come out, those who have done good to *the resurrection of life*, and those who have done evil to *the resurrection of judgment*" (John 5:28-29, emphasis mine).

John the Revelator even describes the resurrection of the damned as a "second death," suggesting that their being raised again will not amount to much:

> "And the sea gave up the dead who were in it, Death and Hades gave up the dead who were in them, and they were judged, each one

of them, according to what they had done. Then Death and Hades were thrown into the lake of fire. This is the second death, the lake of fire. And if anyone's name was not found written in the book of life, he was thrown into the lake of fire" (Revelation 20:13-15).

The lake of fire does not torture but destroys what is thrown into it—or else John would not have written that death and Hades would be thrown into it. John's point is that God will put an end to death, not that he will torture death forever and ever. The same will be true of those thrown into the lake of fire whose names are not found in the book of life.

In contrast, those who attain to the resurrection of life are welcomed into a kind of new Eden, complete with the tree of life we read about in Genesis that will sustains their existence:
> "Then the angel showed me the river of the water of life, bright as crystal, flowing from the throne of God and of the Lamb through the middle of the street of the city; also, on either side of the river, the tree of life with its twelve kinds of fruit, yielding its fruit each month. The leaves of the tree were for the healing of the nations" (Revelation 22:1-2).

Why the Resurrection Is Good News

When discussing this topic with Christians who hold to the eternal conscious torment view of hell, I am often told that utter destruction is not a real punishment; that it is in fact good news for those who reject God. Moreover, only the threat of eternal conscious torment is enough motivation to turn to the God whom one of the authors of scripture described as "my light and my salvation... the stronghold of my life" (Psalm 27:1) and whom Jesus said was the only One who is truly good (Matthew 19:17).

This is news to many of us who are gripped by the fear of death—both our own impending death and the deaths, potential or actual, of our loved ones. The author of the biblical epistle to the Hebrews highlights this deep fear of ours of our own mortality as one of the things that moved Jesus to save us:

> "Since therefore [all human beings] share in flesh and blood, he himself likewise partook of the same things, that through death he might destroy the one who has the power of death, that is, the devil, and deliver all those who through fear of death were subject to lifelong slavery" (Hebrews 2:14-15).

This writer isn't an anomaly. Other ancient thinkers wrote of how we are gripped by our natural fear of death, for instance:

> "Midrash Tanchuma, 'In this life death never suffers man to be glad.' . . . In heathen and savage lands the whole of life is [also] often overshadowed by the terror of death, which thus becomes a veritable 'bondage.' Philo quotes a line of Euripides to shew that a man who has no fear of death can never be a slave."[7]

Chris Date surveyed additional sources,

---

[7] F.W. Farrar, ed. The Cambridge Bible for Schools and Colleges: Volume 51. Accessed via https://books.google.com/books?id=haELAQAAIAAJ

noting the Epicurean philosophers' notion that fear of death prevents people from living happy lives and "nurtures such vices as greed, envy, disloyalty, and injustice." The Epicureans' proposed solution, to foster comfortability with annihilation, ultimately failed to convince their compatriots. Thus:

> "First-century Greek historian Plutarch said his countrymen could not countenance the prospect of annihilation. If given the choice between it and an afterlife of torment, they would have chosen the torment, for 'the Greek loved life and the Greek wanted to live.' The Epicurean project failed, Plutarch wrote, because rather than comforting people, annihilation is the fate 'nature most dreads.' Augustine echoed Plutarch, insisting that if people were given the choice between eternal life in torment and annihilation, 'on the instant they would joyfully, nay exultantly, make election to exist always, even in such a condition, rather than not exist at all.'"[8]

It is plain that human beings fear death. We long to overcome it, to take away its power. Indeed, our fear of death makes us slaves to an impulse to

---

[8] Christopher M. Date, "Dismissive of Hell, Fearful of Death: Conditional Immortality and the Apologetic Challenge of Hell," Hope's Reason: A Journal of Apologetics. Accessed via http://www.stephenjbedard.com/wp-content/uploads/2017/09/HRV6-Hell.pdf

postpone the inevitable. It's why some polytheistic societies offered human sacrifices to appease the gods and thus guarantee a good harvest, why many of us become obsessed with dubious health fads, and why we are often so afraid to take risks in doing the right thing when the right thing might be dangerous.

In contrast, Christian missionaries are known for going to hostile lands to proclaim the good news about Jesus even as they offer medical and hygienic care which both prolongs life and enhances its quality. Christian conscientious objectors like the World War II medic Desmond Doss and non-violent resisters like Corrie Ten Boom and the people of Le Chambon-sur-Lignon put their lives on the line but are unwilling to destroy their enemies. Indeed, the second century Christian bishop Ignatius of Antioch was so unconcerned about the supposed finality of death that he discouraged fellow Christians from interfering with his impending martyrdom at the hands of a hostile Rome.

Of course, this is not to say that believers never fear the process of dying or even have occasional doubts, but our faith in a savior who defeated death on our behalf gives us the confidence to be released from our slavery to the fear of death. The gospel of the resurrection can do the same for anyone who is willing to turn to Jesus and be saved. This good news, that this perishable body will one day put on the imperishable, is the reason why Paul fearlessly stared death in the face, taunting, "O death, where is your victory? O death, where is your sting" (1 Corinthians 15:55)?

Cody Cook

Conclusion

As we have seen, the notion that human beings are inherently immortal simply doesn't line up with scripture. It may be worth noting in the conclusion of our study that it also doesn't line up with any meaningful philosophical conception of an almighty God. Simply put, if the human soul is by definition immortal, God has no ability to destroy it. To say that the human soul must exist eternally is to challenge God's power. If God cannot destroy the creatures He has created, He is no longer the sovereign God of scripture.

But is God truly powerless to annihilate His creation (despite what Jesus said in Matthew 10:28 about fearing the One who can destroy both body and soul in *Gehenna*)? Has He given them a nature like His own so that they possess immortality in themselves (in contradiction to what Paul wrote in 1 Timothy 6:16 about God alone possessing immortality)? And if He has bestowed us all with immortality, to what end did He do it? What would be the point of bestowing immortality on humans that He intends to permanently imprison in a painful lake of fire, thus challenging His own presentation of Himself as a God more merciful than wrathful (see Exodus 34:6-7) and creating a universe where evil will never be totally defeated?

The good news we should be declaring is not about "where your immortal soul is going," but whether or not Jesus defeated death on your behalf.

If our study has shown that the view of unconditional human immortality is both unbiblical and philosophically deficient, why do so many Christians hold to it? Because tradition has obscured our vision and warped the good news we share with the world around us. When we preach a so-called "gospel" of the eternal conscious torment of immortal human souls, we are not preaching the apostles' gospel of the resurrection.

Appendix:
Eternal Punishment and Unquenchable Fire

The purpose of this essay was not to defend conditional immortality (immortality that God grants only on condition of our being united to Christ) at every point, but merely to give a biblical account of it. However, I suspect that many who read this account will have trouble being open to it due to a few biblical prooftexts that they've always understood to teach eternal conscious torment. Keeping this in mind, I have added this short appendix which deals with some of the most common prooftexts for the traditional view of hell.

Eternal Punishment

At the end of a discussion about God separating humanity into two categories at the final judgment, Jesus gives this description of their separate fates:
> "And these will go away into eternal punishment, but the righteous into eternal life" (Matt 25:46)

Robert Peterson, a theologian and defender of the traditional view of hell, offers this deduction from the verse: "The punishment of the lost in hell is coextensive to the bliss of the righteous in heaven—both are everlasting."[9]

While Peterson seems to think this argument is a straightforward refutation of conditionalism, it has some hidden premises. For instance, why does the punishment being everlasting necessarily mean that its recipient must be conscious for it? As Paul said, the wages of sin is death. Jesus Himself contrasts the eternal punishment with eternal life—implying that the punishment is the opposite of the reward, which is life. Isn't it plain that a death which lasts forever is not experienced consciously?

---

[9] Robert Peterson, Annihilation or Eternal Punishment? Accessed via https://www.ligonier.org/learn/articles/annihilation-or-eternal-punishment/

The Gospel of the Resurrection

No conditionalist would object to the notion that the punishment of the second death for the wicked is everlasting. If it weren't, then the damned could come back to life yet again after the second death.

Indeed, there is no reason to assume with the traditionalist that eternal (*aionios*) must *always* mean a *conscious* experience of infinite duration. In fact, there are a number of examples in the Bible which demonstrate that it shouldn't.

For instance, in Jude: "Sodom and Gomorrah... serve as an example [of the fate of the damned] by undergoing a punishment of eternal fire" (Jude 1:7). Here, Jude uses "eternal fire" to refer to what the people of Sodom and Gomorrah suffered. It is clear that Sodom and Gomorrah are not still burning, so Jude must mean something else by "eternal" than literally burning forever. It is exegetically acceptable, and also contextually quite warranted, to understand Jude to be saying that the *consequences* of the fire, not its duration, are eternal.

Peter, who may have borrowed from Jude here, or vice versa, also uses Sodom and Gomorrah as an example for what happens in hell, but with language that supports conditionalism in a much more straightforward fashion:
"by turning the cities of Sodom and

Gomorrah to ashes [God] condemned them to extinction, making them an example of what is going to happen to the ungodly" (2 Peter 2:6).

It becomes clearer now to see how Jude means that those who will end up in hell will suffer eternal fire—the effects of the fire are eternal, irrevocable, unchangeable. As Peter says, those who suffer it are "condemned... to extinction."

This use of eternal as pointing to consequences and not ongoing duration can be seen elsewhere in scripture; for instance in Hebrews 9:12, where it is stated that when Jesus entered "once for all into the holy places . . . [He secured] an eternal redemption" for us. How is it that our redemption can happen at one moment in time but also take place over the course of eternity? It can't. But a redemption obtained once for all *can* have lasting consequences—thus we *were* redeemed and will live out eternity as a redeemed people (see also Isaiah 45:16 and Mark 3:29).

Unquenchable Fire

Sometimes in apocalyptic literature we encounter language which transcends the literal, communicating plain truth using fantastical and hyperbolic language. For instance, the book of

The Gospel of the Resurrection

Daniel foretold that the kingdom of God would supplant the kingdoms of men—but not quite as directly as that. Instead it speaks of fantastic beasts being slain and of statues made of mixed metals being taken down by a rock not made from human hands.

In other words, sometimes passages about God's judgment invoke language which, if understood literally, would not match the historical facts on the ground.

For instance, the prophet Isaiah, in his oracle about God's judgment on the nation of Edom, wrote of unquenchable fire:
> "Night and day it shall not be quenched; its smoke shall go up forever. From generation to generation it shall lie waste; none shall pass through it forever and ever" (Isaiah 34:10).

Leaving aside the obvious discrepancy between a place being perpetually on fire and it lying in waste (which suggests that the fire has completed its work) Edom has obviously not undergone eternal fire. Isaiah only meant that the punishment would be permanent. That's apocalyptic literature for you.

Ezekiel 20:47-48 offers us another example of apocalyptic language, this time with Judah in

mind:
> "Thus says the Lord God, Behold, I will kindle a fire in you, and it shall devour every green tree in you and every dry tree. The blazing flame shall not be quenched, and all faces from south to north shall be scorched by it. All flesh shall see that I the Lord have kindled it; it shall not be quenched."

Ezekiel's meaning is clear—the fire cannot be stopped by anyone; it cannot be quenched. However, this fire will also utterly consume everything it touches. When it is said that the fire cannot be quenched, the claim being made isn't that it lasts forever, but that it can't be put out by human means—it will burn until it's done its work (see also Jeremiah 17:27).

Let's do one more. Isaiah 66:24 speaks of new creation after final judgment, contrasting the state of the people of God from the state of the damned:
> "And they shall go out and look on the dead bodies of the men who have rebelled against me. For their worm shall not die, their fire shall not be quenched, and they shall be an abhorrence to all flesh."

This verse is a go to for traditionalists looking to support eternal conscious torment on the basis of its description of unquenchable fire—but why do these traditionalists ignore the rest of the verse with its description of corpses (NASB), dead bodies (ESV, NIV), or carcasses (KJV)?

Apocalyptic Language in the New Testament

You might have noticed that these Old Testament passages have parallels in the New Testament. For instance, Jesus exhorts His hearers in Mark 9:47-48:

> "And if your eye causes you to sin, tear it out. It is better for you to enter the kingdom of God with one eye than with two eyes to be thrown into hell, 'where their worm does not die and the fire is not quenched.'"

While it's *possible* that Jesus is using the language of Isaiah with a meaning that is different than Isaiah, we should assume that the original context of the passage He's quoting controls, at least to some extent, the meaning of His words as well. If Isaiah's unquenchable fire and unkillable worms grow fat on dead bodies—not on supernaturally perpetually preserved living human beings—it is reasonable to assume that Jesus' do also.

Here's one more New Testament passage that uses this language. It comes from the book of

Revelation, perhaps the most famous example of apocalyptic literature in all of history. The verse concludes a discussion of the mark of the beast and the punishment for those who receive it:
> "And the smoke of their torment goes up forever and ever, and they have no rest, day or night, these worshipers of the beast and its image, and whoever receives the mark of its name" (Revelation 14:11).

While the New Testament is full of quotations and allusions to the Old Testament, the book of Revelation is absolutely steeped in it. The language of unquenchable fire and smoke going up forever is clearly borrowed from Isaiah and Ezekiel. Therefore, any proponent of eternal conscious torment theology citing this verse as a debate ending prooftext without dealing with the original meaning of the words in Isaiah and Ezekiel is mishandling the text of scripture.

Conclusion

While there are more arguments made for eternal conscious torment and innate human immortality than can be addressed in this short volume, it is my hope that the positive biblical case made in the main text and the counter arguments made in this appendix will give the reader confidence in the apostolic proclamation of the resurrection gospel. If you would like to learn more about the conditionalist perspective, I would recommend these additional books:

Fudge, Edward
<u>The Fire That Consumes</u>

Date, Christopher et al.
<u>Rethinking Hell</u>

Fudge, Edward & Peterson, Robert
<u>Two Views of Hell</u>

Finally, I can't recommend enough the website www.rethinkinghell.com. Its podcast, articles, and Facebook group make it an excellent resource for someone who is looking to study this topic out thoroughly for themselves.

About the Author

Cody Cook is a theology graduate student and film buff living in Cincinnati, Ohio with his wife Raven, daughter Ava, and cats Jobyna and Buster.

His other books, articles, and podcast can be found at www.cantus-firmus.com

Other works by Cody Cook available on paperback, Kindle, and at www.cantus-firmus.com...

A Second Adam:
How the Doctrine of Recapitulation Helps Make Sense of the Atonement

Post-Enlightened:
Reflections on Two Hundred Years of Anti-Christian Writing from Thomas Paine to Richard Dawkins

Fight the Powers:
What the Bible Says About the Relationship Between Spiritual Forces and Human Governments

Open Source Jesus:
A Manifesto for a Liberated Church

Printed in Great Britain
by Amazon